The Smallest
Hint

TULSA

ISBN: 9781-954095-91-5
The Smallest Hint

Yorkshire Publishing
1425 E 41st Pl
Tulsa, OK 74105
www.YorkshirePublishing.com
918.394.2665

Printed in Canada

The Smallest Hint

9/2022

Photographs and Poems by
David Jennings

He washed his hands and sat to rest,

Looking out on what he'd done—

The earth and waters coalesced

Against a newly-dying sun

And creatures swarmed the soil and seas

And soared across the sprawling skies

And somewhere—hidden by the trees—

Man awoke and rubbed his eyes.

Like one expectant after prayer:
Hands steadied on the keys,
I sit—submissive—in my chair
And wait for words like these
To come together, set just so,
In ordered fashion—thus—
And question what we cannot know
Or ask what comes of us.

Last I saw you, under snow,
Not more than a month ago
I would have sworn your flowering through—
Gone your red, yellow, blue.

Now, I see your colors—all—
Brighter than they were in fall,
Showing what you could not show
Last I saw you, under snow.

Ocean meets the land,
Waves break down and hiss—
Pushing at the sand,
Dragging back like this.

Shells tumble to shore,
Some stay where they're tossed—
Others, like before,
Roll back and are lost.

Far out in the blue
Goes a little boat—
And the bottle, too,
With my childhood note.

Turn the earth
Toss the seed,
Pray for birth
Pull the weed.

Curse the draught
Pray for rain,
Then pull out
Weed again.

Out here under open sky
An intermittent bird
Tells me what it's like to fly,
In eager, warbling word—

Then, as quickly, flaps its wing
And rises from my bough—
Dipping down and circling
As if to show me how.

May I pick a flower, Sir,
Growing on your grave?
Did you even know there were
Flowers for you to have?

My little girl would love one
Fashioned in her hair,
Set up like a little sun
Just above her ear.

Oh! But that would be one less
Little joy for you,
If—with all that dirt and grass—
Any makes it through.

The train that took me down the track

(I did not have the time to pack)

Consoled me with its click and clack—

I knew I was not coming back.

What light there was from sunset died

While on and on that whistle cried

And pushed my thoughts of life aside

Despite how hard I tried—I tried.

So long that boring whistle blew

Then not—and all the motion, through.

I stood, unsure of what to do,

And stepped out into someplace new.

I held you for a season
As high as I could show—
Adored among the trees, and
Then I let you go.

One by one I dropped you down,
Though sometimes—in a gust—
Basketfuls from my crown
Were mercilessly thrust.

By May, my roots pretended
To hold you, but they—too—
Soon saw their hubris ended
By wind that lifted you.

I held you for a season,
Mine not to ask God why:
Receive, return—his reason.
You bud. You bloom. You die.

Tough, the roadside, sun-drenched flowers,
Dry, the meadow grass,
Low, the clouds that hold the showers—
Slowly moving past.

Tired, my feet must rest from going,
Raw, my tongue and throat—
Long, the road behind is growing,
Harsh, the blackbird's note.

Spent, I drop—the end proclaiming,
Knowing it's not mine for naming.

Looming, you can see the clouds
In rising fashion grow,
Heaped up tall like billowed smoke
Hung over hills below.

Slow, at first, the windmill turns,
But faster, faster still—
Trees shift and the curtains swell
And thrash the windowsill.

Thunder cracks the evening calm,
Fierce lightning splits the sky!
Rain falls—then the rumbled voice
Of God bids his goodbye.

It could have been the wind I guess—
That whisper in the field
I thought at first some hushed address
From God, some truth revealed.

It might have been a grosbeak song—
Such joy, I took to be
An angel singing all day long
Its chirruped tunes to me.

But then again, I've never heard
The wind with such repose,
Nor whistled song from any bird
Heaven and Earth transpose.

He must have stayed up all night long—

That boy out in the tree

Whistling his leaf-blown song

And dropping one, two, three,

Four, five—and six—his acorns down

To smack them off my roof

And scare me—this far out from town.

Go check the yard for proof!

One had dropped its petals, all—
One kept full display,
Like one had resigned to fall
And one wished to stay.

Not long until the cold winds,
Not long until frost.
Then, the emptied stem bends—
Every petal lost.

Surely, I would hold mine late,
Right up to the freeze!
Though—if facing awful fate,
Or some slow disease?

If I could put a ladder up
Against a sturdy tree
Somewhere back in the deepest wood
Where no one else would be,
I'd climb the rungs and grab the trunk
And work to make my way
As high as limbs would let me climb—
A momentary stay.
With all the world below, removed,
And naught above but sky
Save here or there a bird or two
Trying to figure why,
I'd say your name and give you time
To come from where you are—
From depth of space or cloud or wind
Or farthest, faintest star.

Then you and I would share a branch
And likely, first, just stare
A long, slow stare, as if a look
Could somehow keep you there.
And we would laugh and talk and wish
And cry and dread to see
The sun sink ever-slowly down
And down below our tree.
If somewhere this were somehow so
And we could this way meet,
I'd reach that ladder—steadied,
stretched—
And shove it with my feet.

Hear him singing,
Dreadful, low—
See him swinging
To and fro.

Reaping, clearing—
Each cut made,
Feel him nearing
With his blade.

I shot her looking right at me—
Those eyes that, with no word,
Screamed out a startled, helpless plea
To be unseen—unheard—
Unharmed as one in flight from death
Who, having been ensnared,
Would beg release—but with no breath—
Would beg his life be spared.
I shot her—click—and shot again,
Then let my camera down
And prayed her guard from other men
Who come with guns from town.

To walk the winter orchard
With clouds sagged wet in rain,
To see the twisted, tortured
Boughs beg for fruit again.
To know, yet see them pleading,
That spring—that life—will be:
What Christ knew—tired and bleeding—
That walk to Calvary.

Life above begins to die—
Traffic slows and voices fade,
Sunlight sinks below the sky:
Lost. Forlorn. Alone. Afraid.

Angels sometimes talk to me.
Once or twice, I've thought them God—
Walking in waist-high to see
Where the angel feet had trod.

Blanketed, I try to sleep—
Dreams come, but fragmentary:
Immersed in these waters—deep—
Washed in this sanctuary.

Behind the sunflowers—crowded, tall—
Tucked against a silent wood,
Silent too and somehow small:
A shell now where a home once stood.

Then, the porch was run with laughter,
Then, the windows told a tale
Of life and love and ever after—
Then time moved on. Now wrecked. Now frail.

Look long enough—you'll swear you've seen
Movement in an emptied place,
Some soul stuck in the in-between—
Perhaps some once-familiar face.

What once had been—what comes to all:
The sad, uncertain turn to fall.

I heard a distant, little voice
Last night as I slept—
A little, long-lost voice of you
From where dreams are kept.

"Daddy, push me! Push me, Daddy!
Please?" Then, fading, "Please?"
One glimpse—then gone—I saw you, small,
Waiting by the trees.

I woke, and for a moment joy
Was there, near my heart.
Then grief—alone and old and scared—
Away, dark, apart.

I closed my eyes and heard you laugh—
I reached for the swing,
But lost you to the ticking clock,
Constant, deafening.

Someday I might take a drive
And, unseen, disappear:
Somewhere, sometime I'd arrive
A long—long way from here.

Then again, I'm apt to stay,
But dream of where roads go:
This one I might choose today,
And that one—tomorrow.

Now, laid out on the forest floor,
Surrendered, where you stood before,
And absent of your broad décor,
No birdsong fills you anymore—
Nor whistled air of summer wind.
Nor will your needled branches bend
To playing squirrels perched at the end.
No tickled trunk as squirrels descend.

Now, laid out—left for slow decay,
Your limbs outstretched, as if to say
Why does it have to be this way—
As if to ask if I would stay.

A woeful song crept down a stair
And dawdled by a door,
Whistled for someone not there—
A love long-gone before.

I stopped in passing—captured, still —
And listened to the strain:
Forgive, forget, move on until
It all comes back again.

Your door still creaked when I went in,
Your room felt cold and bare—
With everything as it had been
The last night you were there.

Your little shoes. Your comb. Your belt.
Your toys. Your pants. Your shirt.
For every this or that I've felt,
How deep—how raw—this hurt.

I held my breath. I tried so hard
To hear you—if one word!
The only sound came from the yard:
Some cruel, unmindful bird.

Your window still let in the light—
I drew the curtain so
The rest of them—the living—might
Not see me letting go.

Vines compete to take the past,

Claiming stake of boards and nails

Until a tangle has amassed—

Oppressive—and the structure fails.

What happened there—with whom and when—

Stays alive in stories told

Until but one recalls and then

She stops the telling, tired and old.

Most of the time I'm here alone
To watch over the dead.
It's when the mourners come that I—
I have to turn my head.

The early visits are the worst—
They cry and kneel and moan
And grab fistfuls of dirt from where
The bulging pile is thrown.

I've seen them sprawled full on the mound
When no one else was near,
Exhausted—hoarse—from yelling out,
And only me to hear.

In time, they come and simply stand
And look down at the grave,
Mumbling words and plucking weeds and
Flowers they might save.

It's when the mourners come that I—
I have to turn away:
The angst, the grief you could not take!
But I have to stay.

The whisper of the winds through pine,

The gusts that lift the leaves

And swirl them in a whirling line—

Then go like silent thieves.

The distant, shadowed call—one bird—

Whose melancholy air

Is one I think—I know—I've heard

Before, when I was there.

The woods invite me further on,

So further on I go.

Although the light is almost gone,

My way—I think—I know.

Start the raging water's flow,
Twist the trees with moaning wind,
Let the far-off thunder creep.

Brown the summer grasses, slow—
Let the green at least pretend
That their foliage will keep.

Make the lingering leaves let go,
Bring their suffering to an end,
Scoot them to a corner heap.

Hide the world in heavy snow,
Make the rigid branches bend
Under white piled inches deep.

Find me in this box below,
Tell me when I should ascend
From this long, slow, silent sleep.

Worn keys had not been played since when—
Nor hymnal pages turned.
No voice had uttered soft Amen
Nor altar candles burned.

Dust overspread long-empty pews
And lingered in the light
That slanted in—across my shoes—
Through windows to my right.

I thought to leave, not sure that God
Would know me from before:
Defective, disappointing, flawed—
Reject. Disdain. Abhor.

But then—from where—I felt a gust
That breathed across my ear,
Enough to clear a little dust
And calm my soul with fear.

One day a path will lead away

And you—as ought—will go.

You will leave. We will stay.

Life's course is written so.

But keep this spot marked on your chart,

An X to show the place

Where two old people prize—as art—

Each feature of your face.

Tree in snow,
Shadow—light.
Dark below
Mounding white.

Foot tracks gone,
Meadow lost.
On and on
Snowflakes tossed.

Branches bent
Under weight,
Love—lament,
Winter fate.

Of all the things you could have done
You spent your day with me—
Early, bringing the sun to rise
From dark obscurity.

The songbirds woke to your soft nudge
And sang the morning through
In sweet display for me, I thought—
Of course—but no—for you!

Great prairies flowered out by noon
In splatters from your brush—
Your notice raised the sunflowers tall
And made the asters blush.

With evening near, you brought clouds low
To settle in the west
And pushed the sun back down to set
In color—strewn protest.

Of all the things you could have done
You spent your day with me—
Disclosing but the smallest hint
Of vast eternity.